TASTY REACTIONS!

The Chemistry of Food

Written by Joseph P. Cataliotti

WORLD BOOK

www.worldbook.com

Co-published by agreement between Shi Tu Hui and World Book, Inc.

Shi Tu Hui
Room 1807, Block 1,
#3 West Dawang Road
Chaoyang District, Beijing 100025
P.R. China

World Book, Inc.
180 North LaSalle Street
Suite 900
Chicago, Illinois 60601
USA

© 2026. All rights reserved. This volume may not be reproduced in whole or in part in any form without prior written permission from the publisher.

WORLD BOOK and the GLOBE DEVICE are registered trademarks or trademarks of World Book, Inc.

Library of Congress Control Number: 2025942235

Aha! Academy: Chemistry
ISBN: 978-0-7166-7346-0 (set, hardcover)

Tasty Reactions! The Chemistry of Food
ISBN: 978-0-7166-7349-1 (hard cover)
ISBN: 978-0-7166-7369-9 (e-book)
ISBN: 978-0-7166-7359-0 (soft cover)

Staff

Editorial

Vice President
Tom Evans

Senior Manager, New Content
Jeff De La Rosa

Associate Manager, New Content
William D. Adams

Senior Curriculum Designer
Caroline Davidson

Curriculum Designer
Mikayla Kightlinger

Proofreader
Nathalie Strassheim

Indexer
Nathaniel Lindstrom

Graphics and Design

Senior Visual Communications Designer
Melanie Bender

Designer
Shannon Hagman

Written by Joseph P. Cataliotti

Acknowledgments

The publishers gratefully acknowledge the following sources for photography. All illustrations were prepared by WORLD BOOK unless otherwise noted.

Cover: Drazen Zigic/Shutterstock; Erika Anes/Shutterstock; monticello/Shutterstock; Pixel-Shot/Shutterstock; Pravosudov Yaroslav/Shutterstock

© Aziz/Adobe Stock 8; © Dipali S/Adobe Stock 9; © grey/Adobe Stock 46; © Markus Blanke/Adobe Stock 9; © LAYER-LAB/Adobe Stock 34; © New Africa/Adobe Stock 11; © Nomad_Soul/Adobe Stock 37; © Pic_it/Adobe Stock 5; Alabama Extension (licensed under CC0 1.0) 29; © The History Collection/Alamy 17; Francois Lafon (licensed under CC0 1.0) 37; Raysonho @ Open Grid Scheduler/Grid Engine (licensed under CC0 1.0) 39; © AndreyPopov/iStock 27; Jynto (licensed under CC0 1.0) 10, 17, 43; Maja Dumat (licensed under CC BY 2.0) 45; © National Archive 43; Public Domain (Metropolitan Museum of Art) 29; Public Domain 5, 7, 10, 25, 30, 42; © Shutterstock 3, 4, 5, 6, 7, 8, 9, 10, 11, 12, 13, 14, 15, 16, 17, 18, 19, 20, 21, 22, 23, 24, 25, 26, 27, 28, 29, 30, 31, 32, 33, 34, 35, 36, 37, 38, 39, 40, 41, 42, 43, 44, 46, 47, 48; © Steve Zylius/UC Irvine 25; WDnet (licensed under CC0 1.0) 28; Yulo1985 (licensed under CC BY-SA 4.0) 7

There is a glossary of terms on page 48. Terms defined in the glossary are in type that looks like *this* on their first appearance on any spread (two facing pages).

Contents

Introduction 4

① **Food basics** 6
    Lipids 8
    Proteins 10
    Carbohydrates 12

② **Chemistry of taste** .14
    Fake flavors 16
    Fusion flavors 18

③ **Cooking up chemistry** 20
    Browning 22
    You can't unfry an egg 24
    The dangers of cooking 26

④ **Preserving food** 28
    Food gone wrong .30
    Salting, brining, and pickling 32
    Vital molecule: sodium chloride 34
    Fermentation 36
    Freezing 38

⑤ **Baking** 40
    Vital molecule: baking soda 42

Bake some muffins 44
Index 46
Glossary 48

Introduction

Food—everyone needs to eat it, including you. You may even be eating food right now. Try not to get crumbs on the book, though!

There are many different types of food from all across the world, from American cheeseburgers to Chinese wontons. But despite the great variety of foods, all food follows the same rules: the rules of chemistry. That's right, all food has a science to it, even hamburgers.

I have many ingredients!

What is chemistry? Chemistry is the scientific study of the substances that make up everything and how they react with one another. Foods are no exception.

Keep reading to learn about the delicious chemistry of food.

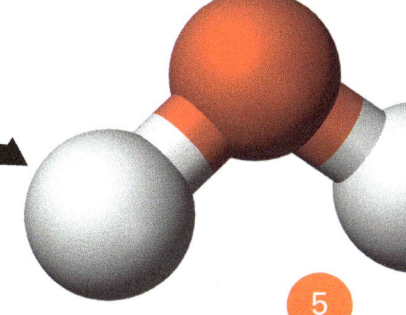

All foods include H_2O, a basic chemical you know as water.

1 FOOD BASICS

Yum, dessert!

While it may be tempting to fill up on sugary desserts, a healthy meal can't just be sweets. People who study nutrition recommend that you eat fruits, vegetables, grains, *protein* foods, and dairy—or a dairy alternative—every day. Why, though? Why is it important to eat all those different foods?

While there are many different types of foods, food scientists group foods based on the substances that make them up. A healthy diet requires a balance of different foods!

It's all about the different *compounds* that make up foods. When you eat food, your body digests it, breaking down the food into different *molecules*. Those tiny molecules are made up of tiny *atoms*, which are the building blocks of all things.

6

Your body needs those molecules to do all the things it does! It also breaks the molecules apart or joins them together in chemical reactions.

Chemical *reactions* are a key part of chemistry. In a chemical reaction, the atoms that form a substance bond together with other atoms or split apart to form a new substance. Here's an example: one molecule of methane (CH_4) and two molecules of oxygen gas ($2O_2$) can come together in a fiery chemical reaction to produce a molecule of carbon dioxide (CO_2) and two molecules of water ($2H_2O$)!

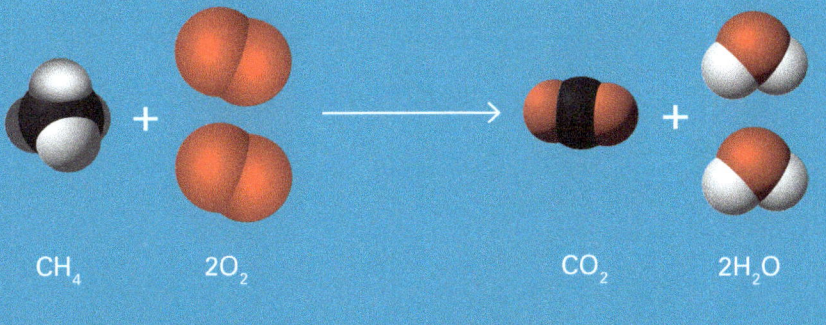

CH_4 $2O_2$ CO_2 $2H_2O$

Keep on reading to see the different types of foods your body needs.

DID YOU KNOW?

A balanced diet also requires vitamins: specialized molecules that the body uses for various purposes. If you don't get enough vitamins, you may become sick.

Vitamin D3

Food basics

Lipids

Such tasty foods as butter and olive oil consist largely of lipids. Lipids are made up of complex molecules that include carbon, hydrogen, and oxygen atoms.

Food is my fuel!

Why do you need lipids?
Lipids are a key source of energy. In a complicated process, your body breaks down lipids and either converts them to energy or stores them for later. Your body also uses lipids in all sorts of important microscopic structures.

***Lipids* are one key substance that everyone needs to eat.** Lipids include animal fats and plant oils.

You may love jumping into a pool, but lipids don't. They're hydrophobic, meaning "scared of water"— that is, they don't dissolve in water. This makes them good for building tiny cellular structures that won't dissolve away!

CURIOUS CONNECTIONS

BIOLOGY A cell's flexible covering, called the cell membrane, is made up of a double layer of lipids called phospholipids. Their hydrophobic tails face toward each other, with the hydrophilic heads face outward. Proteins and other molecules are also embedded in the membrane.

Food basics

Proteins

What exactly are proteins? Proteins are large, highly folded *molecules* made up of carbon, hydrogen, nitrogen, oxygen, and other *atoms*. You can break proteins apart into smaller molecules called *amino acids*.

Myoglobin protein

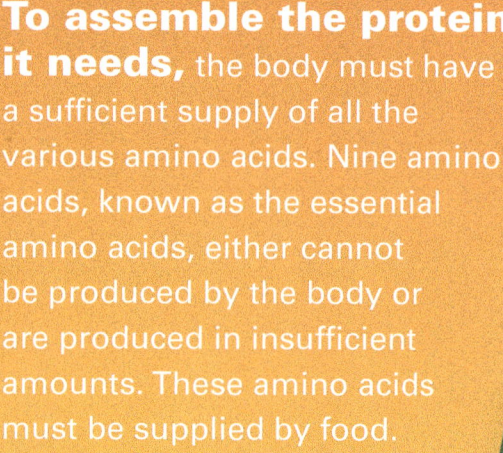

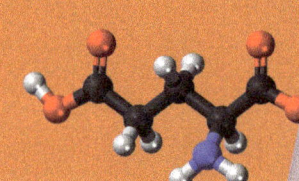

Amino acid

What is an acid? An acid is a special type of chemical that gives up hydrogen atoms when it reacts with other substances. Some acids can even corrode metal, but amino acids are too weak to do so.

To assemble the proteins it needs, the body must have a sufficient supply of all the various amino acids. Nine amino acids, known as the essential amino acids, either cannot be produced by the body or are produced in insufficient amounts. These amino acids must be supplied by food.

Proteins are another key substance that everyone needs to eat. Such hearty foods as meat, eggs, and milk are high in protein.

Alongside meat, eggs, and dairy, protein can also be found in high amounts in other foods. Cereal grains, legumes, nuts, and different types of vegetables also have tasty proteins for you to eat.

After this: lunch.

Why do we need proteins?

Proteins are important in building, maintaining, and repairing human body tissues, especially bone, cartilage, and muscle. Proteins make up a large part of each cell in the body. The body can also burn proteins for energy when necessary.

In addition, every cell contains proteins called enzymes that speed up or make possible chemical reactions. Without enzymes, the cells could not function.

TECH TIME

The proteins in your body do many different things. Scientists have begun to design new proteins for special purposes. This may lead to major advances in the fields of medicine and biology.

Food basics

Carbohydrates

The simplest carbohydrates are sugars, also called saccharides. Glucose is a sugar found in plants and in the human bloodstream. Another sugar is fructose, found in fruit. When single saccharide *molecules*—called monosaccharides—come together, they form polysaccharides. Glucose and fructose combine to make sucrose, which is table sugar. There are other types of sugar, too, such as lactose, found in milk.

Carbohydrates can be found in fruits, vegetables, and grains.

Monosaccharides

Glucose

Fructose

Polysaccharides

Sucrose

Lactose

Some people may try to "cut carbs" to lose weight, but *carbohydrates* are an essential category of foods. Sugars and *starch*, found in bread and potatoes, are carbohydrates.

Molecules of glucose and fructose are made up of rings of carbon along with oxygen and hydrogen atoms. As you may have noticed, a lot of the basic food molecules have these atoms. The key is the ability of these atoms to form molecules of various shapes.

Why do we need carbohydrates? Cells use glucose as fuel for their functions and the building and repair of body tissues.

CAREER CORNER

Do you enjoy learning about molecules? You may want to become a chemist! Chemists can work in a variety of jobs. They study chemical substances or synthesize (make) new substances for many different purposes.

2 CHEMISTRY OF TASTE

DID YOU KNOW?

Scientists have also identified plenty of more specific tastes! Can you think of any more?

Saltiness is another taste. It's caused by *sodium chloride*—salt. Another taste is bitterness, caused by all sorts of chemicals in foods. It might have originated to warn us against unsafe foods.

You taste something when the taste buds on your tongue detect certain chemicals in the food you eat. So, chemistry can explain why foods taste great... or not so great!

Scientists have identified a few basic tastes. Sourness is one taste. *Acids,* such as the citric acid in fruits, produce this taste.

Dumplings are savory.

You may not like bitter tastes, but umami, or savoriness, is generally more popular. Many different molecules can cause this taste, including monosodium glutamate (MSG).

Besides the chemicals in food, other factors, such as temperature, also influence taste. That's why cold food can sometimes taste worse than warm food.

Many people's favorite taste is sweetness. Sugar is the main culprit.

Most foods don't have just one flavor but a combination of flavors. In addition, scientists have devised ways to make flavors using manufactured chemicals. Plenty of foods you eat have artificial flavors!

Chemistry of taste

Fake flavors

One artificial sweetener is saccharin, which a chemist first made by accident in 1879. It's several hundred times sweeter than sugar! Because saccharin has fewer calories than sugar, it's used to sweeten diet foods, such as sugar-free soda and candy. Another artificial sweetener is aspartame, first made in 1965. It's also much sweeter than sugar.

CURIOUS CONNECTIONS

PSYCHOLOGY Psychologists who study human perception used to believe that certain flavors could only be tasted by specific parts of the tongue. This idea soon became widely believed, but experiments have mostly disproven it. In reality, you can taste all flavors all across your tongue.

Because humans love sweet tastes, scientists have invented plenty of artificial sweeteners to add to foods.

Scientists can also synthesize (create) more complex tastes. Vanilla is a common one. Vanillin, the molecule that gives vanilla its unique flavor, is generally extracted from vanilla beans. However, because demand for vanillin is so great, scientists have developed ways to synthesize it. They can, for example, make it using chemicals from the wood pulp or petroleum industries. Chemical *reactions* are the key to turning these substances into vanillin.

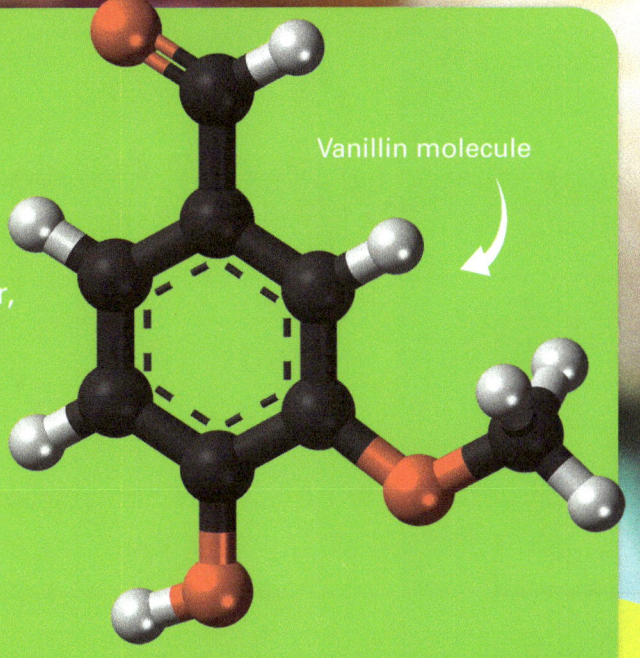

Vanillin molecule

People often hear the word "chemical" and get suspicious, especially when talking about food. But everything is a chemical, including water!

Chemistry of taste

Fusion flavors

Even simple foods can have a complex taste. Apples, for example, get their flavor from many different *molecules.* They have sweet glucose, fructose, and sucrose as well as several *lipids* and *acids.*

Let's look at another food—vinaigrette, a salad dressing.
Basic vinaigrette includes olive oil, vinegar, and lemon juice.

Vinegar is made in a complex process. Liquid from grains or fruits are fermented using yeast, a type of fungus. This process turns sugars into *alcohol* in a chemical *reaction.* Using different bacteria, the alcohol is turned into water and acetic *acid*, which has a sour taste.

Olive oil is made from smushed olives. It has various fatty oils and other *compounds,* giving it a slightly fruity, grassy taste. The acids in lemon juice give a different sour flavor. These tastes all come together in vinaigrette.

The food we eat rarely has just one taste.

Some foods have complex tastes, and chefs have mastered the art of combining different flavors to make new ones.

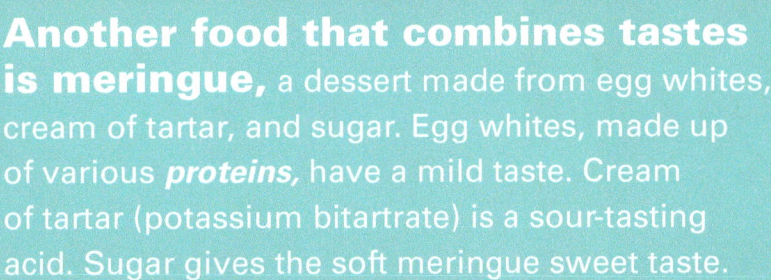

The individual ingredients of vinaigrette are made in chemical reactions, but they don't react chemically to make vinaigrette. There is no vinaigrette molecule. Instead, vinaigrette is just a mixture of the various molecules in its ingredients.

Another food that combines tastes is meringue, a dessert made from egg whites, cream of tartar, and sugar. Egg whites, made up of various **proteins,** have a mild taste. Cream of tartar (potassium bitartrate) is a sour-tasting acid. Sugar gives the soft meringue sweet taste.

CAREER CORNER

Are you interested in combining flavors and making new foods? Believe it or not, professional chefs make a living creating extraordinary food and practicing the culinary arts! That could be your job, too!

COOKING UP CHEMISTRY

Besides killing bacteria and making food easier to digest, cooking food has other important effects on the chemistry of what we eat.

Cooking food can save lives! Uncooked food can have harmful bacteria and other organisms.

Cooking egg whites causes the highly folded **proteins** to unwrinkle, then form new structures. Along the way, the white turns from a runny liquid to a jiggly gel. This process, called coagulation or gelation, is one reason why eggs are widely used in baking.

Applying heat to your food causes all sorts of complicated chemical *reactions*. Don't apply too much heat, though. You don't want to burn your food—or start a fire!

Browning

A couple of different chemical reactions explain why food turns brown when you cook it.

When you fry up a juicy steak, the meat turns from red to brown. It happens because the cow muscle tissue has a *protein* called myoglobin that is reddish in color. When cooked, the protein *molecules* change and become brown-colored.

Another browning reaction is called caramelization. It happens with sugars. When we cook sucrose, eventually it breaks apart into glucose and fructose. Then, those sugars break apart further, forming a whole bunch of different molecules. This process darkens the food and gives it a nutty, buttery taste. Caramelization is used to make tasty caramel candies.

When you cook food, it often turns brown. It's a chemical *reaction* in action, right before your eyes!

Yet another reaction is called the Maillard reaction. Most foods tend to have simple sugars, such as glucose, and amino groups from *amino acids* or proteins. When we cook these molecules together, a complex chemical reaction begins that makes large, brown molecules. It also releases all sorts of aromas and *compounds* with delicious tastes. The Maillard reaction especially boosts the savoriness of food. The delicious taste of cooked meat, for example, is caused in large part by the Maillard reaction. Yum!

Bon appétit!

The chemist **Louis Camille Maillard** was the first to realize how widespread this chemical reaction was, back in the early 1900's. That's how it became known the Maillard reaction.

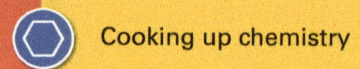
Cooking up chemistry

You can't unfry an egg

As an old saying goes, you can't unfry an egg. But why not? Frying an egg breaks down the egg *molecules* and makes new ones, including brown char through the Maillard reaction.

You'd have to reverse each complicated chemical reaction, which is basically impossible! Cooking an egg also untangles all the wrinkly egg *proteins* and forms new structures, which is why eggs turn from gloopy to spongy when you cook them.

Some chemical *reactions* are reversible, meaning they can be undone. However, many important chemical reactions cannot be undone in any practical way, including those used in cooking. So cook carefully!

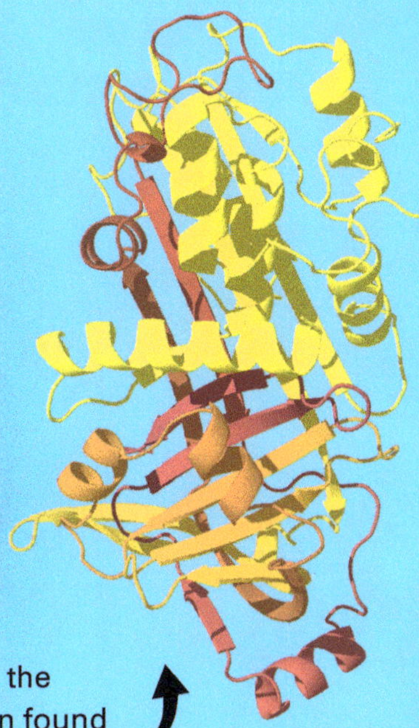

Ovalbumin, the main protein found in egg whites

TECH TIME

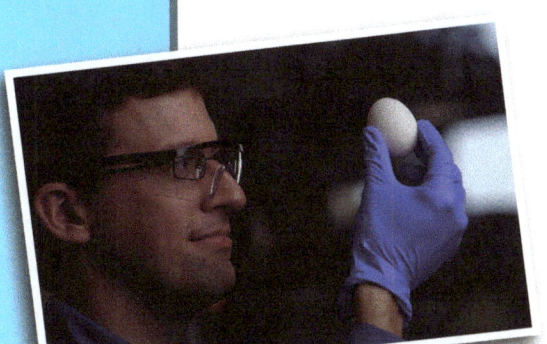

While it's basically impossible to unfry an egg, scientists have actually found a way to unboil one! Because boiled eggs aren't charred, scientists just have to worry about refolding the eggs' proteins. By dissolving the boiled egg and spinning it in a tube very fast, they can do just that. It may seem like a wacky idea, but it could have some use in medicine.

25

Cooking up chemistry

The dangers of cooking

Hot grease or oil isn't just a fire hazard. If people aren't careful, they can accidentally burn themselves, too. It's important to be careful in the kitchen.

Edible oil is used to cook food. If it gets too hot, it may begin to smoke at about 400 °F (200 °C), depending on the type of oil. That's called the smoke point!

Why does oil smoke? The heat begins to break down the oil's fat *molecules,* producing airborne particles. This smoke is bad for people, but most cooking is done below the smoke point.

Cooking doesn't always go right.
Careless cooking can even result in a kitchen fire! Kitchen fires are a particular risk when people cook using oil or grease.

If oil continues to heat and there's an ignition source, like a lit flame, vapors of the oil can catch fire. That's called the flash point. At an even higher temperature, the oil can catch on fire without a source of ignition—that's called the fire point. These temperatures depend on the molecular make-up of the oil. Soybean oil, used by restaurants to deep fry tasty French fries and other foods, has a flash point of around 600 °F (300 °C).

DID YOU KNOW?

One reason why oil fires are so dangerous is that people don't know how to put them out. In a panic, people often reach for water, but water is a horrible way to put out a grease fire. The water will not put out the flames but instead splash flaming grease all over, spreading the fire. Grease fires should be handled by smothering the flames, for example by putting a lid on the pan, using a kitchen fire extinguisher, or calling for professionals if the fire gets out of control.

4
PRESERVING FOOD

If you don't preserve food, the food may rot or liquefy. Yuck! Luckily, human beings have come up with many different ways to preserve food.

Some ways are better for some foods, while other ways are better for others.

Preserving food makes it possible to transport food great distances to your kitchen. That's how you can enjoy cheese from France, carrots from Mexico, or salmon from Norway.

One preservation method is putting food in a can. In canning, food is sealed in airtight containers, then heated to destroy any harmful microbes already in the can. People can all sorts of foods, including soup and vegetables, and ship them great distances.

28

We humans have been preserving food for eons, since before we invented writing! Prehistoric people probably dried grains, nuts, fruits, roots, and other plant products in the sun. People who lived in cold climates likely kept food outside their caves or huts in the winter to prevent spoilage. In warmer climates, people probably stored foods in caves and other cooler places.

Another method uses salts or acids to prevent harmful organisms from growing on old food.

Refrigeration and freezing are yet more key ways to preserve food. Cooling food prevents microbial activity and slows down deterioration. You may have a fridge in your house, but there are also refrigerated trucks that transport food. Brr!

Preserving food

Food gone wrong

Food can go bad three different ways. The first is biological, the second is chemical, and the third is physical.

Biological deterioration happens when harmful *microbes*—such as bacteria, molds, and yeasts—grow on food. Have you ever left bread or fruit out too long? You might have noticed mold. Mold is a type of fungus and is very often not safe to eat. *Eew!*

Chemical deterioration includes *reactions* that turn fruit brown. This might sound like the Maillard reaction, but fruit can turn brown without even being cooked—think mushy old banana peels or apple slices. This process is called enzymatic browning, because it happens when enzymes in fruits react with the oxygen in the air. While the Maillard reaction tends to result in tasty new *molecules*, enzymatic browning tends to make the fruit taste worse. Yuck!

If you leave food out for too long, it can spoil. Spoiled food not only tastes bad, but it's also dangerous!

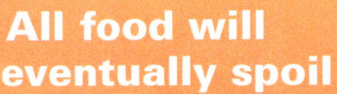

All food will eventually spoil if not preserved. Some foods, such as nuts and grains, can be stored for months with almost no treatment. Other foods, such as milk and meat, stay fresh only one or two days without preservation. The time that a particular food can be maintained in edible condition is called its shelf life. Preservation can extend a food's shelf life, but not indefinitely.

Physical deterioration includes food being crushed or melted, for example newly purchased ice cream that gets left in a hot car. Oops!

DID YOU KNOW?

Not only does preserving food prevent it from spoiling, but it also keeps a fresh flavor! That way, the bread you eat isn't stale and the frozen vegetables you roast are still delicious.

Preserving food

Salting, brining, and pickling

Salting is an ancient way to preserve food.
Ancient people salted meat and fish to prevent spoiling. But how does this work? Salt draws water out of food, preventing such *microbes* as bacteria, yeast, and mold from multiplying.

More bacon, please!

Meats and fish are preserved with salt in a process called curing.
Often curing also involves chemicals called nitrates and nitrites, as well as *sugar* and spices for flavoring. When you cure pork with salt, sodium nitrite or potassium nitrite, sodium phosphate, and sugar, you make bacon!

Food can also be preserved by covering it in salt, nitrates, or *acid*. Not only does this prevent food from rotting, it also can improve the taste of the food.

You can make pickles by brining (soaking them with salt and acid) such vegetables as cucumbers, carrots, olives, or peppers. The acid can be produced by bacteria through a process called *fermentation.* Acid can preserve foods by creating an environment in which harmful microbes cannot grow. Food makers also might add acids to the product. Those acids are what makes pickles taste so sour!

Preserving food

Vital molecule: sodium chloride

STATS

Chemical formula

NaCl

Melting point
1473.3 °F (800.7 °C)

Boiling point
2669 °F (1465 °C)

Salt consists of the elements sodium and chlorine. Its formula is NaCl, so there is one sodium atom for every chlorine atom. These atoms join together in a gridlike pattern to form crystals.

Salt usually forms clear crystals that are almost perfect cubes. However, impurities in the salt may make it appear white, gray, yellow, or red.

***Sodium chloride* is one of the most important chemicals in the world,** especially for us humans. You may know it best as... salt!

Salt is necessary for good health. Human blood contains salt. Your cells need salt to function properly. Some studies have suggested that too much salt or other sodium compounds in a person's diet can lead to high blood pressure. For this reason, many people attempt to reduce the amount of salt they eat. Some people use salt substitutes that do not contain sodium.

Much of the table salt purchased by consumers is also iodized. That means it has potassium iodide or sodium iodide added to it. A lack of iodine in a person's diet can result in a condition called goiter, in which the thyroid gland becomes enlarged. Not good! But, just a small amount of iodine is enough to prevent goiter. Thanks, salt!

DID YOU KNOW?

On average, Americans eat about 3,400 milligrams (mg) of sodium per day. That's much more than is recommended: 2,300 mg!

Preserving food

Fermentation

What exactly is fermentation? It's a biological process in which **microbes,** such as bacteria, molds, and yeasts, break down organic materials in the absence of oxygen. That might sound gross, but most foods made by fermentation are perfectly safe. However, some fermentation can be harmful. For example, fermentation in meat can result in a deadly food poisoning called botulism.

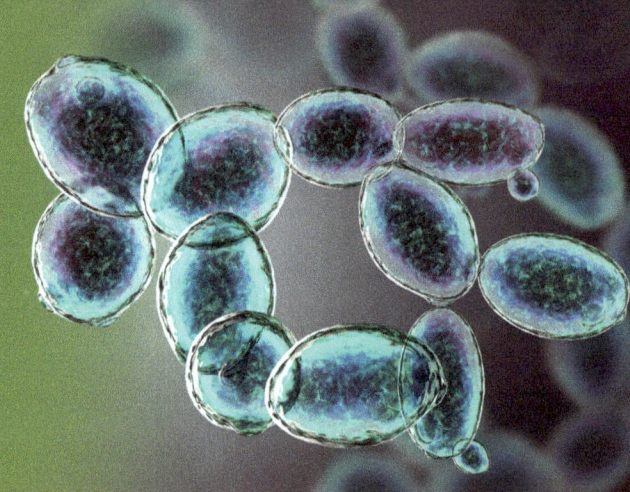

How does fermentation preserve food? Food-makers might add *acid* to food to preserve it, but acid can also be produced by acid-making bacteria in the food itself! That's part of the process of fermentation. So, in contrast to other preservation methods, fermentation actually encourages the growth of certain kinds of bacteria. The bacteria most often used in fermented foods produce acetic acid or lactic acid that wipes out harmful microbes. This is how we make kimchi, salami, sauerkraut, sour cream, vinegar, and many cheeses.

Do you like yogurt, cheese, bread, or chocolate? You have *fermentation* to thank!

Fermentation is also how the drinkable *alcohol*, called ethanol, is made. First, workers fill tanks with liquid rich in **carbohydrates** and other nutrients. Then, they let microbes ferment the nutrients. In beer brewing, yeast consumes *sugar* from malted grain, turning it into carbon dioxide gas, heat, ethyl alcohol, and small amounts of other *compounds*.

> Chance favors only the prepared mind.

People have used fermentation to make alcoholic beverages for ages. But, scientists did not discover how microbes cause fermentation until the 1800's. At that time, the French biologist **Louis Pasteur** studied fermentation in wine. His work advanced the French wine industry and led to a better understanding of foodborne illness.

Preserving food

Freezing

Freezing prevents microbial activity and slows down enzymatic deterioration. Although most foods contain large amounts of water, food freezes differently than pure water. The solutes (dissolved **sugars** and salts) in foods reduce their freezing point to lower than 32 °F (0 °C). Typically, foods begin to freeze at around 31 to 28 °F (−0.5 to −2 °C). Frozen foods are stored at or below 0 °F (−18 °C).

Vegetables are often preserved by freezing. Before freezing, vegetables are first blanched (briefly scalded in boiling water). Blanching prevents enzymes from changing the flavor and texture of vegetables during frozen storage. Other foods preserved by freezing include fish, juices, meat, and poultry. Before freezing, food may be cleaned, peeled, or prepared in other ways. Some foods are even cooked! Some frozen entrees are cooked before freezing.

Brr! Freezing is a great way to store food. Just don't store frozen food for too long, or else it can get freezer burn!

Sometimes food even tastes better when it's frozen, because it may be preserved better. You can store food for a long time in a freezer, then heat it up without much issue. Usually...

Food can get freezer burned. When food isn't properly wrapped or frozen, chilly water molecules can sublimate, or turn to vapor, and escape from food. This leaves food dehydrated and damaged. Freezer-burned food is safe to eat but not as tasty!

5 BAKING

Wheat flour is a superstar in baking. Flour's *proteins,* when mixed with a liquid, form a sticky, stretchy substance called *gluten.* Gluten gives strength and structure to baked goods.

Besides flour and such liquids as water or milk, most doughs and batters need a little help from leavening agents. Yeast, *baking soda,* and baking powder are common leavening agents. When you start heating up your dough, leavening agents create carbon dioxide gas in a chemical reaction, puffing up your dough like tiny, inflating balloons in a stretchy network of gluten.

You have chemistry to thank for delicious baked goods. Such ingredients as flour, yeast, and water come together in chemical *reactions* to make scrumptious bread.

Heating up dough also causes solid fats to melt and spread out. In pie crusts and croissants, layers of spread-out fat create a flaky texture. Gases in the dough also expand, stretching or lifting the product. Then, proteins in the flour become firm, and **starches** in the flour absorb water, giving the finished product structure.

Finally, moisture on the outside of the batter or dough evaporates. This evaporation allows a browned crust to form in the Maillard reaction.

 Baking

Vital molecule: baking soda

STATS

Chemical formula

NaHCO$_3$

Decomposition
120–500 °F
(50–270 °C)

Soluble
1 in 10 parts water
at 77 °F (25 °C)

Baking soda is an important ingredient in baking. It's also known as sodium bicarbonate, or NaHCO$_3$. It has one sodium *atom,* one hydrogen atom, one carbon atom, and three oxygen atoms per *molecule.* These molecules come together to form crystals.

 +

Sodium ion   Bicarbonate ion

If you like bread, biscuits, and pastries, you have *baking soda* to thank. Baking soda causes these goods to puff up while baking.

Baking soda is used in baking powders.
Such powders also include **starch** and **acid**-forming ingredients. The starch keeps the powder dry and prevents it from acting until a liquid is added. Baking soda reacts with the acid-forming ingredient to produce carbon dioxide gas. Yet another chemical **reaction!**

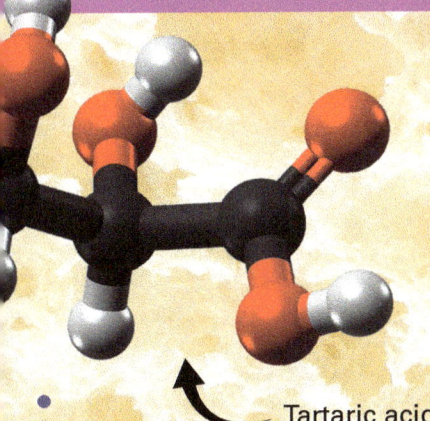

Tartaric acid

Different kinds of baking powders contain different acid-forming ingredients.
Tartrate baking powders contain cream of tartar and tartaric acid as acid-forming ingredients. Phosphate powders have calcium dihydrogen phosphate. Sulfate powders contain sodium aluminum sulfate, or alum. Combination, or double-acting, powders have phosphate and sulfate. These different chemicals react at different speeds, changing the baking process.

Science is very beautiful.

Baking soda isn't just good for baking. It can also remove pesky stains. In the **Manhattan Project** to produce the first nuclear bomb, scientists used baking soda to remove dangerous uranium dust from clothes.

43

Bake some cookies

You will need:

- 2 cups all-purpose flour
- 3 teaspoons baking powder
- ½ teaspoon salt
- ¾ cup white sugar
- 1 egg
- 1 cup milk
- ¼ cup vegetable oil

You will also need a measuring cup, a muffin tin, paper liners, and an oven, too.

You can add additional ingredients, like chocolate chips or blueberries, if you like! The boundaries of chemistry (or in this case, baking) won't ever be advanced without experimentation.

Give it a try

1. Preheat your oven to 400 °F (200 °C).
2. As the oven heats up, grease your muffin tin or insert the paper liners.
3. Pour the flour, baking powder, salt, and white sugar into a large bowl.
4. Then, stir! As you do, try to remember what you learned about these different ingredients.
5. Crack the egg into either a different bowl or your measuring cup. Then, pour in the milk and vegetable oil.
6. Whisk together those ingredients.
7. Once they're well mixed, pour them into the flour mixture, and mix together. Now your muffin mix is ready!
8. Spoon this mixture into your muffin cups so that each is about three-fourths full.
9. When your oven is ready, slide your tin into it. It should take about 25 minutes—or until the muffin top is slightly springy—for the muffins to be done.

Now that you've learned so much about the chemistry of cooking, it's time to apply your knowledge! Let's bake some muffins! Be sure to ask an adult for help, because you're going to be using the oven.

Try this next!

Why not try your hand at some other foods? There are plenty of cookbooks and recipes available in your local library or online. But don't forget to ask an adult for help. Who knew chemistry could be so tasty!

QUESTION TIME!

Can you remember all the different chemical processes we learned that go into making these muffins? What do you think would happen if we removed one of the ingredients, such as egg or flour or baking powder? How would your muffins be different? How do all these ingredients come together to make a delicious treat?

Index

A
acetic acid, 18, 36
acids, 10, 14, 18-19, 23, 29, 33, 36, 43
alcohol, 18, 37
amino acids, 10, 23
aspartame, 16
atoms, 6-8, 10, 13, 34, 42

B
bacteria, 18, 20, 30, 32-33, 36
baking soda, 40, 42-43
bitterness, 14
boiling, 25
brining, 32-33
browning, 22-23, 30

C
canning, 28
caramelization, 22
carbohydrates, 12-13, 37
carbon, 8, 10, 13, 42
carbon dioxide, 7, 37, 40, 43
chef (career), 19
chemical reactions, 7, 11, 17-19, 21-25, 40, 43
chemistry (career), 13
chlorine, 34
citric acid, 14
compounds, 6, 18, 23, 35, 37

curing, 32

E
enzymes, 11, 30, 38

F
fats, 9, 18, 26, 41
fermentation, 18, 33, 36-37
fire, 21, 26-27
freezing, 29, 38-39
fructose, 12-13, 18, 22
frying, 22, 24, 27

G
glucose, 12-13, 18, 22-23
gluten, 40
grease, 21, 26-27

H
hydrogen, 8, 10, 13, 42

I
iodine, 35

L
lactic acid, 36
lactose, 12
lipids, 8-9, 18

M
Maillard, Louis Camille, 23
Maillard reaction, 23-24, 30, 41
Manhattan Project, 43
methane, 7
microbes, 28-30, 32-33, 36-38
mold, 30, 32, 36
molecules, 6-7, 13, 34-35, 42-43
monosodium glutamate (MSG), 15
myoglobin, 10, 22

N
nitrates, 32-33
nitrites, 32
nitrogen, 10

O
oil, 26-27
olive oil, 8, 18
oxygen, 7-8, 10, 13, 30, 42

P
Pasteur, Louis, 37
phosphates, 32, 43
pickling, 32-33
proteins, 6, 9-11, 19, 21-25, 40-41
psychology, 16

R
refrigeration, 29

S
saccharin, 16
salt, 14, 29, 32-35, 38
savoriness, 15, 23
sodium, 14-15, 32, 34-35, 42-43
sodium chloride, 14, 34-35
see also salt
sourness, 14, 18-19, 33, 36
spoilage, 29, 31-32
starch, 13, 41, 43
sucrose, 12, 18, 22
sugar, 12-13, 15, 18-19, 22-23, 32, 37
sulfates, 43
sweetness, 15-19

T
tartar, cream of, 19, 43

V
vanilla, 17
vanillin, 17
vinaigrette, 18-19
vinegar, 18, 36
vitamins, 7

Y
yeast, 18, 30, 32, 36-37, 40

Glossary

acid (AS ihd)—a type of molecule known by its special properties; it gives up a hydrogen atom in reactions

alcohol (AL kuh hawl)—a type of molecule, often carbon atoms, that has a hydroaxyl group, or a duo of oxygen and hydrogen

amino acid (uh MEE noh AS ihd)—a type of acid that makes up proteins

atom (AT uhm)—an incredibly tiny particle that makes up all things

baking soda (BAY kihng SOH duh)—a compound that creates carbon dioxide gas when heated

carbohydrate (KAHR boh HY drayt)—a type of molecule that is the main source of energy for animals and plants

compound (KOM pownd)—a group of many of the same molecule

fermentation (FUR mehn TAY shuhn)—a biological process that breaks down organic materials in the absence of oxygen

gluten (GLOO tuhn)—a substance made up of proteins that gives dough its elasticity

lipid (LIHP ihd)—a type of molecule that does not dissolve in water and is a source of fuel

microbe (MY krohb)—a microscopic organism, not all of which are bad

molecule (MOL uh kyool)—a group of joined atoms

protein (PROH teen)—a type of molecule made up of amino acids that is essential for life

reaction (ree AK shuhn)—a process by which one or more substances are converted into one or more different substances

sodium chloride (SOH dee uhm KLOHR yd)—a clear, brittle mineral called salt

starch (stahrch)—a carbohydrate found in the living cells of green plants

sugar (SHUG uhr)—a sweet-tasting carbohydrate found in plants

www.ingramcontent.com/pod-product-compliance
Lightning Source LLC
Chambersburg PA
CBHW061255170426